# VICTORIAN
# ILLUSTRATED MUSIC SHEETS

Lyrics of songs and ballads had been printed on single sheets for sale in England since the invention of letterpress in the 15th century, sometimes with an appropriate woodcut image added by the printer. The earliest known English sheet music with an engraved illustrated cover is the collection called *Parthenia,* the first music printed for the virginals in 1611. Throughout the 18th century, and indeed to the present day, music was commonly reproduced by engraving on copper (and later, pewter and zinc), because this was a much more flexible method than printing music with metal types. Illustrations could easily be engraved on the copper plates, along with the musical notation, so in the second half of the century music sheets were often produced with ornate head-pieces or half-page illustrations, as in the celebrated collection by Bickham, *The Musical Entertainer* (1736-1739).

From about 1800 the method of engraving known as aquatint was used for these illustrations, and although this produced delicate results imitating water-colour, it was an expensive process in which the copper plates quickly wore out. Since aquatint was not used for printing the musical notation, these illustrations occupied a full page which became the cover to the music. Thus the aquatint cover marked the development from the 18th-century half-page title image to the 19th-century illustrated music sheet. Steel engraving gradually took over from copper from about 1820, but its results produced harsh images. The most

important development in the history of sheet music printing was Senefelder's invention of lithography.

Lithography was introduced into England about 1800, and was first used for printing sheet music illustrations from about 1820. 'Drawing on stone' or 'polyautography', as it was first known, is based on the principle that grease repels water while limestone will absorb both grease and water. A design drawn with wax or crayon on a stone, which is then washed with water, may be inked with a roller and only the design will retain the ink. This may then be printed. At first the sheets printed by this method were coloured by hand, but after the patent for colour lithography was taken out in 1837, music publishers soon began using this new technique for their titles. Coloured illustrations could now be published more cheaply and in far greater numbers than had hitherto been possible.

Several artists in the 19th-century specialised in designing music cover illustrations, and although many covers are not signed, the characteristic styles of the best artists may often be recognised. Maxim Gauci (1774-1854) produced many engraved and hand-coloured sheets which earned him the title of 'father of music hall artists', and his work certainly influenced that of John Brandard (1812-1863). Brandard illustrated a series of waltzes and polkas that the showman composer and conductor Louis Jullien began publishing from about 1844. Chromolithographs by Brandard were remarkably subtle, smooth and even in tone; he took great care in preparing his lithographic stones correctly and ensured that his illustrations were printed on high quality paper. While Brandard's work may be recognised by its delicate colouring and sophisticated portraiture, that of his successor Alfred Concanen is noted for its witty represent-ations of London scenes and characters (page 23). Concanen (1835-1886) was perhaps the most versatile and prolific of all the Victorian music illustrators. In the 1870s he executed line drawings on a regular basis for *The Illustrated Sporting and Dramatic News,* and also illustrated books. Concanen's gift for observation and his inclusion of humorous details probably influenced the work of H.G. Banks, who worked with him when they were both producing illustrations for the litho-graphic firm Stannard and Dixon. Banks enjoyed using inset roundels and vignettes in his covers which illustrated several verses of a song (page 29). He produced many covers for the publishers Francis Day and Hunter (established 1877), and was working at a time when the quality of music sheet illustration was generally in decline.

In all the music covers in this selection, the image is dominant and the lettering is subordinate, purely to give essential information about the title, singer, lyricist, composer and publisher. Some artists tried to incorporate suitable lettering in their designs, as may be seen in the illustrations for *The Doris Waltz* (page 21) and *At Trinity Church I Met My Doom* (page 31), where 'rustic' lettering echoes the shapes of the branches and twigs. But by the turn of the century, new letterforms were popular and the image began to lose its supremacy. Ornate, bold and mixed letterforms which had appeared on playbills and broadsides in the second half of the 19th-century, began to overpower the illustrations on music covers. By the 1890s publishers could reproduce photographs of singers and composers on the covers by the new method of photolitho-graphy, and, once this was possible, colour lithograph illustrations seemed very old-fashioned. The most popular music sheets at the turn of the century featured a photographic image or two, surrounded by a selection of the novel letterforms. Just as technical innovations in lithography had encouraged the rise of the Victorian illustrated music covers, so, paradoxically, technical innovations heralded their decline. By 1900 this type of music sheet cover was rarely produced, although music sheets themselves continued in popularity past the demise of the Music Hall, c.1918, and well into the 1950s.

The demand for sheet music was tremendous in Victorian Britain and the illustrated covers proclaimed the singer and the song in a colourful and appealing way, much as the record sleeves of today advertise the records within. A most important factor in the popularity of sheet music was the rise of the Music Hall 'star' or 'lion comique'. Performers such as George Leybourne, Arthur Llyoyd, G. H. Macdermott and Alfred Vance (pages 12 & 13), could command salaries as high as £100 a week, and were idolised like the pop singers of today. Both the subject matter and the popularity of illustrated music sheets is closely associated with the rise of the Music Halls which opened their doors in the 1850s and 1860s. Their precursors were the 18th-century Tavern entertainments and the early 19th-century Song and Supper Rooms, whose profits came from the price of the food and drink, the entertainment being provided free of charge. The publican Charles Morton visited three of the most successful Song and Supper Rooms in the 1840s — Evans's, The Coal Hole, and The Cyder Cellar, and on their lines opened the first real Music Hall in 1849, in a former public house called the Canterbury Arms. Initially Morton did not admit ladies to his Music Hall, and as in the Supper Rooms, there was no admission charge; but when he opened his new Canterbury Hall in 1852, entry was by a sixpenny refreshment ticket and ladies were welcomed. One great early 'star' of the Canterbury was Sam Collins, an ex-Irish chimney sweep whose greatest success was the song *Limerick Races.* Collins always carried a shillelagh on stage and wore a 'caubeen' or soft felt hat with his green coat, whipcord knee breeches and worsted stockings, as shown in Maguire's illustrations to the *Limerick Races* music sheet (page 8). Later he too went into Music Hall management, opening Collins's in Islington in

VICTORIA & ALBERT MUSEUM

*Catherine Haill*

Theatre Museum, V&A

LONDON: HER MAJESTY'S STATIONERY OFFICE

© Crown copyright 1981
First published 1981
ISBN 0 11 290355 X

COVER: Illustration from music sheet cover for *Hangelina!*
sung by Edward Terry in *Jeams,* Gaiety Theatre, 26 August
1878. Words by F. C. Burnand, music by Meyer Lütz.
Colour lithograph, signed Alfred Concanen. Enthoven
Collection.

Printed in England for Her Majesty's Stationery Office
by Colorgraphic Ltd, Leicester
Dd 696373 C 100

1862, a popular hall which held about a thousand people.

The success of the Canterbury encouraged Charles Morton to build the most grandiose Music Hall yet seen — the Oxford, which opened in March 1861 and cost over £35,000 to build. Its splendid corinthian pillars and special star-shaped gas chandeliers are depicted in *The Oxford Galop* music cover by Thomas Packer (page 9), and although it was by no means as cosy as its predecessors, the emphasis was still on good variety entertainment for patrons who could eat and drink at tables near the stage. As in other contemporary theatres, there was always danger from the gas lighting, cigarettes and overcrowding, and the orginal Oxford was destroyed by fire in 1868. Many similar incidents occurred in the following years, and by 1878 a law was passed demanding that all Music Halls possessed a Certificate of Suitability. Those proprietors who could not afford to install the necessary safety curtains and proscenium walls were forced to close, and in those that remained open the sale of alcohol was banned in the auditoria. Thus the Music Halls that survived were more like 'straight' theatres than the early Song and Supper Rooms, and they gained some respectability at the end of the century from the patronage of the Prince of Wales.

Another reason for the increasing popularity of music sheets in the mid-19th-century was the introduction of the upright piano about 1827. It was small enough to be accommodated in the parlours of modest homes, and its early acquisition denoted a certain status to envious friends and neighbours. Possession of a television set aroused similar feelings a hundred years later, and like that more passive instrument of home entertainment, the upright pianoforte was soon a feature of many homes. Jullien's quadrilles, polkas, mazurkas and waltzes were purchased for home performance during the 1840s, but by the 1860s and after, the greatest demand was for copies of songs popularised by the great stars of the Music Hall.

When pianomania began to spread among the middle classes in the 1840s, devotees of the new fashion demanded an increasingly wide selection of music sheets. These were, however, comparatively expensive, and, at a time when the average weekly wage was about £3, it was not those who paid 6d for an evening's entertainment with food and drink at the Music Halls who could afford to spend 2/6d or 3/- on one music sheet. The mazurkas, polkas and waltzes were tame enough to be played by the most sensitive child learning the piano, but her father might have bought copies of the racy songs sung by Leybourne and Vance to amuse his friends after dinner. He would not have visited the Music Halls, particularly in their early days, but the publication of the songs performed there made a rather risqué form of entertainment available to a much more 'respectable' audience. Music publishing became a very lucrative business, and by 1888 there were nearly a hundred music shops in London. A popular song could sell as many as 80,000 sheets and the publishers had low outgoings. They often used poor quality paper and paid very low fees to the lyricist and composer. In the 1860s and 70s an artist may have commanded as much as £20 for one cover illustration, since the publishers realised that a good illustration by a popular artist could sell thousands of sheets of the most mediocre music, but the lyricist would have had to be satisfied with about £5. The music was sometimes adapted or pirated at no charge at all, and there were no strict regulations about copyright or royalties until 1882.

The following selection of illustrated covers indicates the wide range of subjects covered by Victorian sheet music. Plays, actors, and actresses gave rise to music and song, as did current events, famous people and places, and (inevitably), love, courtship and marriage. *Mazeppa Waltzes* (page 10), inspired by the popular play of that name, is illustrated with a dramatic image of the equestrian performer Adah Isaacs Menken at the point in the play where she is strapped to a horse in her scanty costume and pursued by a pack of wolves. Menken first played the part in London at Astley's Theatre in 1864, and died in Paris four years later at the age of thirty-three. A more domestic scene from a successful musical drama by Planché is depicted in Concanen's cover for Quadrilles from *Babil and Bijou*, first performed at Covent Garden Theatre in August 1872 (page 14). *The Lights O' London Galop* (page 23) is another theatrically-inspired piece, first performed at the Princess's Theatre in 1881. Concanen's representation of a cobbled London street faithfully depicts the jostling scene with its ubiquitous barrow boys, the central one selling baked potatoes (and ice cream!) from his 'can' or oven on wheels. Concanen obviously enjoyed depicting such scenes and their characters; his illustration for *The Piano Girl* (page 19) shows a gypsy-clad street entertainer with her piano organ, another familiar sight in 19th-century London. The artist W. George has clearly been influenced by Concanen in his representation of a city street scene in his cover *How London Lives* (page 32), another song from a play — this time a melodrama at the Princess's Theatre, 1897. In contrast to these street scenes, *The Doris Waltz* (page 21), is illustrated by a contrived theatrical scene from the comedy opera at the Lyric Theatre in 1889.

A good illustration of a popular 'star' was perhaps the best means of selling a song sheet. Music Hall singers and comedians were closely associated with their 'hit' songs whose titles could even establish catch phrases or new words such as 'zoo'. This abbreviation was quickly adapted by the British public, much to the horror of the Royal Zoological Society, after the success of Alfred Vance's song *Walking in the Zoo* in 1870 (page 13). Dan Leno (1860-1904), the great cockney Music Hall star, features on the cover of *Our Stores Ltd* (page 24), and his friend and successor Harry Randall (1860-1932) is depicted complete with comic whiskers and ill-fitting evening dress on *I Mustn't Let Her See Me All At Once* (page 27). The familiar comic features of George Robey — 'the Prime Minister of Mirth' (1869-1954) — are seen on Banks's cover for Robey's first hit song *The Simple Pimple* (page 29), while Lottie Collins is depicted high-kicking her way through her enormously successful song *Ta-Ra-Ra-Boom-Der-Ay* on the music sheet of that name (page 30).

Lottie Collins achieved fame through this song which she first sang in 1891 in the pantomime *Dick Whittington*, and later commanded as much as £200 a week singing it in America.

The New Police Force of 1829, the Great Exhibition of 1851, the delights of drinking various brands of champagne, and even the Victorian vogue for the gorilla in the 1870s — all such topical events were immortalised by Music Hall songs, and merited illustrations on the sheet music covers. London Pleasure Gardens feature on the covers of music sheets, and Concanen depicts a typical scene from either Highbury Barn or Cremorne pleasure gardens on his cover for *The Brokin 'Arted Butler* (page 12). The new sport of Polo which was first played in England at Hounslow between the Ninth Lancers and the Tenth Hussars inspired the *Polo Lancers* (page 17), again illustrated by Concanen. Many sports featured on music covers, while in contrast the fashionable Aestheticism with its penchant for peacock feathers, sunflowers and anything Japanese, was also satirised. Music Hall performers poked fun at this movement mercilessly, as we see on two more of Concanen's beautifully detailed illustrations for *Quite Too Utterly Utter* (page 21) and *My Aesthetic Love* (page 22).

The delicate problems of romance and wedlock gave rise to many popular Music Hall songs, and were fruitful topics for amusing illustration. *My Aesthetic Love* (page 22) depicts a hopeful suitor visiting his Pre-Raphaelite sweetheart, and Harry Randall's comic song *I Mustn't Let Her See Me All At Once* (page 27), concerns the difficulties of making a favourable impression on a new girl-friend! Husbands have long lamented disagreeable mothers-in-law, as shown in *I Can't Stand Mrs Green's Mother* (page 18), while *At Trinity Church I Met My Doom* (page 31) illustrates Tom Costello's song that rues the day he ever walked down the aisle!

By the beginning of the 20th-century, when contemporary music sheet covers were mostly typographical, a few collectors began to appreciate the old style of lithographed cover more on account of their covers than for the songs and music they contained. The illustrations, depicting the miriad topics dealt with by the songs, were seen to be accurate and topical reflections of the dress, surroundings and atmosphere of the previous century. The first book on illustrated music titles was published privately by the author W. E. Imeson in 1912; in it he predicted accurately that 'sooner or later, the old picture-cover will be recognised by that arbitrary mistress of arts, Dame Fashion. Then, as something to collect, it will be generally sought after'. Rather less wisely, Imeson advocated removing the music and keeping only the illustration which he then suggested should be trimmed down for mounting and framing without the title and names, which could be noted on the back of the mounts. The collector today would do well not to heed Imeson's well-meaning advice, but the sheets are now more scarce and expensive than they were in 1912.

Victorian illustrated music covers reflect an era, as well as a popular form of entertainment. Many of the songs depicted are still well-known, while those forgotten are evoked by their covers. Although the 1890s witnessed the decline of the illustrated music sheets, in the previous fifty years they had reigned supreme, like the colourful songs they adorned: 'with immense success and great éclat'.

SUNG WITH GREAT ECLÁT.
BY
SAM: COLLINS,

Sam Collins (1826-1865). Music Hall artist. From illustrated music cover to *Limerick Races.* Colour lithograph signed Harry Maguire. Enthoven Collection

Oxford Music Hall. Built for Charles Morton and opened 1861. Destroyed by fire
1868. From an illustrated music cover to *The Oxford Galop*. Colour lithograph signed
T. Packer. Enthoven Collection

*Mazeppa Waltzes* Illustrated music cover. Colour lithograph signed R. J. Hamerton
H. R. Beard Collection F148-5

*The Music Man,* sung by Howard Paul in his 'afternoon entertainments'. Illustrated
music cover. Colour lithograph signed Concanen Lee & Siebe del et lith.
H. R. Beard Collection F43-39.

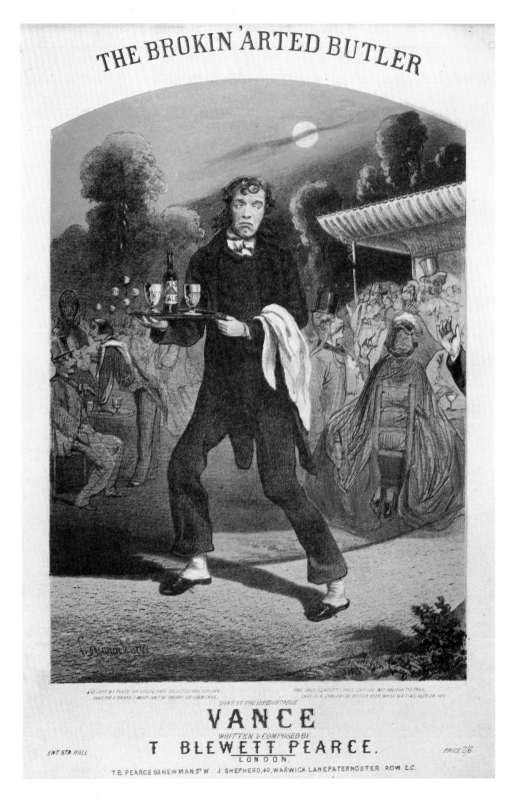

*The Brokin 'Arted Butler*, sung by Alfred Vance (The Great Vance). Illustrated music
cover. Colour lithograph signed Concanen & Siebe. Enthoven Collection.

Alfred Vance (The Great Vance) (1840-1889). Music Hall artist. Illustrated music cover to *Walking in the Zoo* which Vance first sang in 1870. Colour lithograph signed Rich^d Childs. Enthoven Collection.

Arrangement of quadrilles from *Babil and Bijou*, musical drama by Dion Boucicault and
J. R. Planché. Theatre Royal Covent Garden 19 August, 1872. Illustrated music
cover. Colour lithograph signed Alfred Concanen. Enthoven Collection.

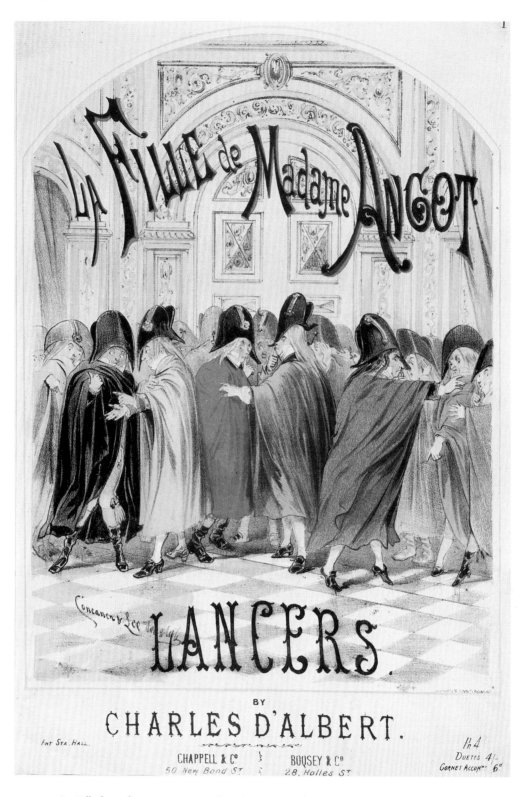

*La Fille de Madame Angot Lancers* by Charles d'Albert. Illustrated music cover. Colour
lithograph signed 'Concanen & Lee del & lith'. H. R. Beard Collection
F133-37.

*Mrs Partington's Private Theatricals.* Illustrated music cover. Colour lithograph signed
Alfred Concanen. Enthoven Collection.

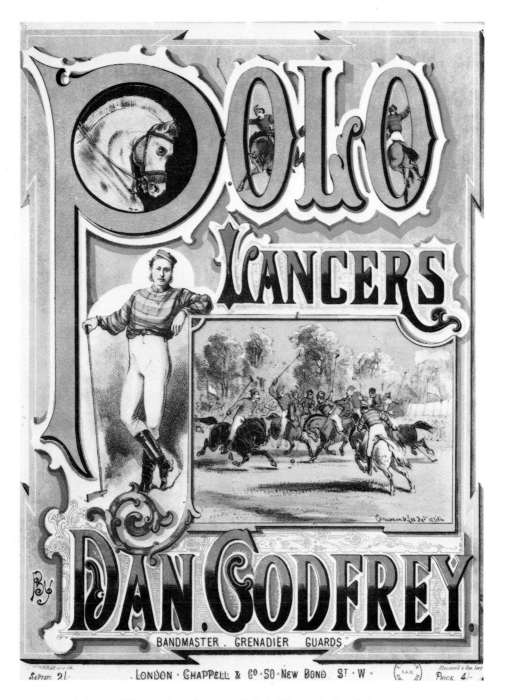

*Polo Lancers.* Illustrated music cover. Colour lithograph signed Concanen & Lee.
Enthoven Collection.

18

*I Can't Stand Mrs Green's Mother,* sung in London Music Halls c.1878-1880. Illustrated
music cover. Colour lithograph signed Alfred Concanen.
Enthoven Collection.

*The Piano Girl,* sung by Fred Coyne in London Music Halls c.1879. Illustrated music cover. Colour lithograph signed Alfred Concanen. Enthoven Collection.

*Billee Taylor*, quadrille on airs from the comic opera by H. Pottinger Stephens and Edward Soloman. Imperial Theatre 30 October, 1880. Illustrated music cover. Colour lithograph by Thomas Packer. Enthoven Collection.

*Quite Too Utterly Utter.* Roundelay satirising the aesthetic movement of the 1880s.
Illustrated music cover. Colour lithograph signed Alfred Concanen.
Enthoven Collection.

*My Aesthetic Love or Utterly Utter, Consumate Too Too.* One of the numerous songs
satirising the aesthetic movement of the 1880s. Illustrated music cover. Colour
lithograph signed and dated Afred Concanen 1881. Enthoven Collection.

Galop from *The Lights O' London,* play by G. R. Sims, Royal Princess's Theatre, 10 September, 1881. Illustrated music cover. Colour lithograph signed Alfred Concanen. Enthoven Collection.

Dan Leno (1860-1904) Music Hall artist. Illustrated music cover to *Our Stores Ltd.*
Colour lithograph. H. R. Beard Collection F42-17.

Arthur Roberts (1852-1933). Music Hall artist. Illustrated music cover to *T'aint Natural* sung by Roberts in the burlesque of *Robinson Crusoe*, Avenue Theatre 23 December, 1886. Colour lithograph signed H. G. Banks.
Enthoven Collection.

*Not Really*, sung by Harry Nicholls and Herbert Campbell in the pantomime *The Forty Thieves*, Drury Lane 27 December, 1886. Illustrated music cover. Colour lithograph signed H. G. Banks. Lith. H. R. Beard Collection F40-54.

Harry Randall (1860-1932) Music Hall artist. Illustrated music cover to *I Mustn't Let Her See Me All At Once.* Colour lithograph signed Cee Tee. H. R. Beard Collection F153-46.

Waltz from *Doris,* comedy opera by B. C. Stephenson and Alfred Cellier, Lyric 20
April, 1889. Illustrated music cover. Colour lithograph signed H. B.
Enthoven Collection.

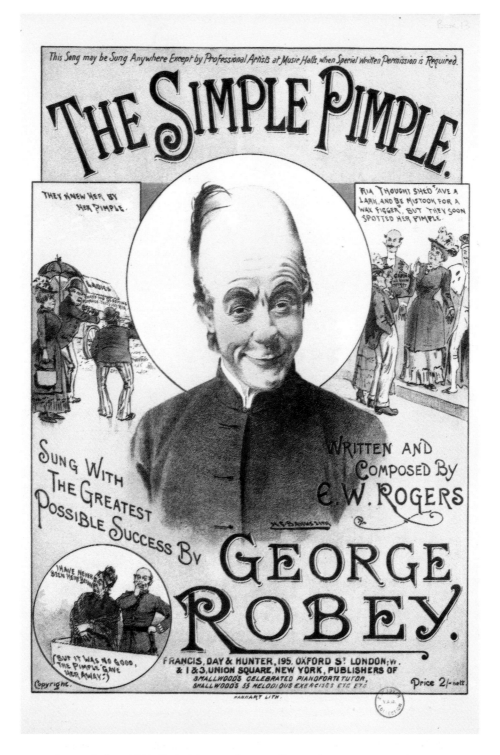

George Robey (1869-1954). Music Hall artist. Illustrated music cover to *The Simple Pimple,* Robey's first hit song. Colour lithograph signed H. G. Banks. Enthoven Collection.

Lottie Collins (1866-1910). Music Hall artist. Illustrated music cover to *Ta-Ra-Ra-Boom-Der-Ay,* her most famous song, which she popularised in 1891. Colour lithograph. H. R. Beard Collection F153-30.

*At Trinity Church I Met My Doom.* March comique after the song made popular by
Tom Costello in 1894. Illustrated music cover. Colour lithograph by H. G. Banks.
Enthoven Collection.

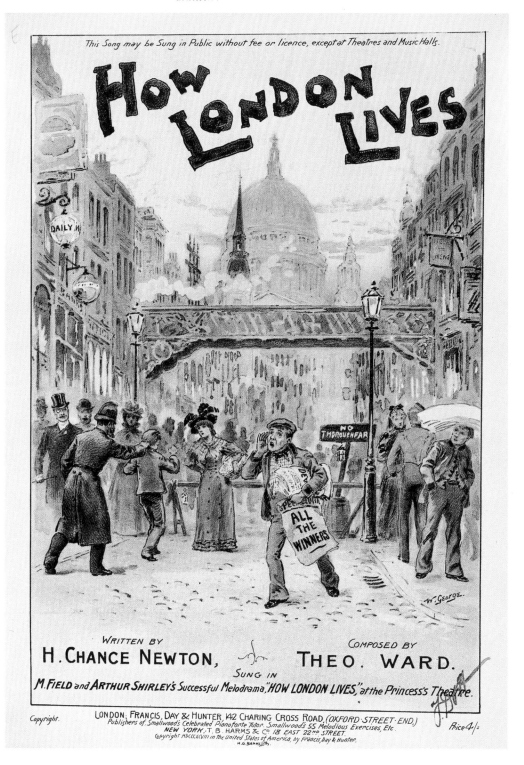

*How London Lives*, song from the melodrama of the same name by Martyn Field and
Arthur Shirley. Princess's Theatre 27 December, 1897. Illustrated music cover. Colour
lithograph signed W. George. Enthoven Collection.